JAMESTOWN EDUCATION

THE CONTEMPORARY READER

VOLUME 1, NUMBER 2

D0979961

Mc Graw Hill Glencoe
McGraw-Hill

New York, New York   Columbus, Ohio   Chicago, Illinois   Peoria, Illinois   Woodland Hills, California

CONTENTS

ALL KINDS
OF
CATS

Of all the big cats, tigers are the best swimmers.

Why were cats once burned alive?

1   To some people, a cat means beauty and grace. To others, a cat means mystery or power. Cats have held a special place in people's lives for thousands of years.

TRAITS IN COMMON

2   Except for size, all cats are much the same. All are very strong for their size and move in much the same way. They can be fast and mean. Most can fish. All cats can swim. Some don't really like water unless there is no other way to escape.

3   Most cats can climb. All have good sight, hearing, and smell. All have pads on their feet with sharp claws under them. They kill quickly, so they are great hunters.

AN OLD FAMILY

4   No one knows when the first cat lived. But the most famous cat of long ago is the saber-toothed tiger.[1] During the Ice Age,[2]

---

[1] saber-toothed tiger: large cat of long ago with long, curved upper teeth

[2] Ice Age: a time long ago when ice covered most of the Earth

this cat moved into all parts of the world. It died out many, many years ago.

Cat lovers have been breeding special varieties of cats for about 100 years.

5   Cats were part of every family in Egypt 5,000 years ago. They were pets, but they also killed the mice and rats that ate stored grain. People even got their cats to fish and hunt for them. The people of Egypt saw their cats as gods. When a cat died, its owner made it a mummy. In the 1800s, a graveyard just for cats was found in Egypt with mummies of 300,000 cats.

6   People of the Middle Ages[3] were afraid of cats. They believed that cats held the power of black magic. So they began to kill them. They burned them alive in the center of town. Over time, there weren't enough cats left to kill mice and rats. Rat bites made people very sick. Many people died because there were not enough cats.

CLOSE TO HOME

7 By the 1700s, cats were again friends and mice killers. Today there are about 30 million pet cats in the United States.

8   A little more than 100 years ago, there were no cat breeds.[4] Then people began mating the cats they liked best. A certain color, ear shape, or leg size was passed down over the years. These became breeds such as Siamese [Sy•uh•meez'], Persian [Per'•zhun], and Manx [Manks]. Clubs around the world help people keep the breeds pure and also start new breeds.

---

[3] Middle Ages: the time in Europe's history from about A.D. 500 to A.D. 1500
[4] breeds: groups of plants or animals that are related by family lines and that have like traits

Jaguars are great leapers and among the fastest runners of the cat family.

TIGERS

9 The biggest wild cat in the world is the tiger. Tigers live in China and other parts of Asia. They are found in no other parts of the world, except in zoos.

10 There are different kinds of tigers, but all have black stripes on a yellow or orange body. The tiger's tail has black rings. A male tiger may weigh as much as 500 pounds and be 10 feet long. Three feet of his length is his tail.

11 Tigers are big, strong, and fierce. They like to hide in the jungle or in thick brush along a river. Tigers can swim better than any other cat. They may walk around during the day to see what's in the area. Then at night they go hunting. Tigers will kill cows, horses, sheep, and goats. They will kill almost any kind of wild animal. But tigers won't go after elephants or bears for fear of getting killed first.

Most leopards have black spots on tan bodies. Those that are black all over are called panthers.

LIONS

12 Lions and tigers act much the same. Their bones look alike. They are about the same size. When a lion and a tiger mate, their offspring is called a liger. Lions and tigers are different in that the lion has no stripes. Also, the male lion has a mane. Most lions stay with their mates for life.

13 Lions also hunt at night, in pairs or groups. The team goes out looking for a zebra, giraffe, or other animal. The female lion hides near a water hole. The male lion scares the animal with his loud roar. The female then jumps on it and bites deeply into its neck. The male keeps up the loud roar. When the animal is dead, he joins the female to feed.

14 Lions and tigers kill people only if they can't go after animals. That can happen if their teeth or claws are broken. It can happen also when they are too old and slow to hunt wild animals.

Lions and tigers are closely related. But tigers live in Asia, and lions live in Africa.

Cats make delightful pets and can quickly train humans to wait on them.

OTHER FAMILY MEMBERS

15 A leopard may be as long as a lion or tiger. But it has spots and weighs less than 200 pounds. The leopard climbs trees. It jumps long and high. It lives in Asia and Africa.

16 The hunting leopard of India is the cheetah. It can run at speeds of up to 70 miles per hour. That is faster than any other land animal.

17 The jaguar is the leopard's cousin. It is the biggest cat in Central and South America. The jaguar is six or seven feet

long. Not many jaguars are left. They are in danger of dying out.

18   A smaller leopard cousin is the ocelot [ah'•suh•laht]. It weighs 25 to 35 pounds and has both stripes and spots. Some are still found in both the United States and Mexico.

19   Big or small, each kind of cat is important to other living things. The largest tiger helps balance life in the wild. The smallest house cat can brighten the life of a person. Whatever their role, cats are special in our lives and our world. ♦

QUESTIONS

1. In what ways are all cats alike?
2. How did the people of ancient Egypt feel about cats?
3. Which cat is the best swimmer?
4. Which cats hunt in pairs or groups?

SPEEDY, SILENT, SAFE & STYLISH

POPE Waverley ELECTRIC

MODEL NO·36 PRICE $900. WITHOUT TOP $850.

The above picture shows the latest, lightest and speediest electric runabout ever built. In this model we have fully realized our aim to bring out an electric runabout which would be a leader both in design and equipment. The forward box design is distinctive and contains a compartment suitable for carrying the storm aprons, side curtains, and small packages. This model is fitted with 30 cells of No. 28 Sperry or 30 cells of 7 PV Exide batteries, giving a light battery equipment.

We make Runabouts, Surreys, Stanhopes, Chelseas, Physicians' Road and Delivery Wagons and other models.

POPE-WAVERLEYS ARE "ALL-THE-YEAR-ROUND" VEHICLES.

Buy now and enjoy the late summer and fine autumn riding.

Complete catalogue and address of our depot in your vicinity on request.

POPE MOTOR CAR COMPANY,   -   Indianapolis, Ind.

A 1904 ad for an electric car promises all the latest features for comfort and performance.

Are you getting choked up over gas fumes?
Perhaps it's time for another kind of car.

Electric Cars

1   Try to think of life without cars. It's not easy. But our cars make us sick. Their exhaust pollutes[1] the air. Dirty air is hard to breathe. On some days in large cities, the air is thick and gray. Polluted air drifts all over. It even rises high above Earth. Many scientists feel that it can change the weather. Everyone is hurt by pollution.

2   Each day there are more cars, buses, and trucks. Each day they cause more pollution. We can't get rid of our vehicles. But we can change them. Their gasoline engines are the problem. Vehicles could be powered some other way. A likely form of

---

[1] pollutes: makes impure

Early electric cars were quiet and clean, but they were slow and couldn't go far.

energy is electricity. Today, researchers are trying to build a useful electric car.

3   The electric car is not a new idea. The first electrics were made about 100 years ago. In fact, three kinds of engines were used on early cars.

EARLY ELECTRICS

4 Around 1900, thousands of cars ran on electric batteries. They were silent, so they never scared horses. They were clean. They were easy to start. Almost every woman driver chose an electric car.

5 But electric cars were slow. Their top speed was 20 or 30 miles per hour. Going uphill, top speed fell to 4 or 5 miles per hour. Even worse, they couldn't go far. After about 30 miles, the batteries had to be recharged.

Some Progress

6 Other cars had steam engines. A steam-powered car was almost as clean as an electric. And it was much faster. Racing steamers reached speeds of over 100 miles per hour. With normal use, steamers ran at 30 miles per hour for more than 150 miles.

Drivers liked steam-powered cars better than electric cars because they were faster.

Self-starters instead of cranks made gas-powered cars more popular after 1912.

7   Cars with gasoline engines also went fast. And they had a wider range. Refueling took only minutes. As long as a car could get fuel, its range had almost no limits.

8   But these gasoline-powered cars had drawbacks. There were many moving parts that could break. They often did. A driver had to fix many things on, in, and under the car. Driving one of these cars could be dirty. Worst of all, the engine had to be cranked before the car would start. Only a strong person could do that.

9   Then, in 1912, the self-starter came into use. Now an electric battery, not a

crank, would start a gas-powered car. Suddenly, these cars were as easy to start as electrics. They were already as fast as steamers. Both the electric car and the steamer began to lose ground. Within 20 years, no one made them anymore.

MODERN ELECTRICS

10 In the 1960s, attention turned once more to the electric car. What could increase its speed and range?

11 Some researchers looked at the lead-acid battery. They tried new designs. They tried different materials. Some batteries they made were better than those of today. But the strongest ones cost too much.

12 Other researchers worked on a slightly different power source. It is called a fuel cell. A fuel cell could be twice as strong as a lead-acid battery. But, even today, it is too heavy and costly.

13 Recharging was also studied. Drivers wouldn't mind stopping so often for a recharging if it took only minutes. Still

Modern electric cars are on the drawing board and the test track.

another idea was to design a lighter car. Then a regular battery could push it faster and farther.

14   Today, many designs are being tested. Large and small companies and even people on their own are building electrics. Reports say that work is moving ahead.

ROAD TESTS

15 One owner tried to drive cross-country in his modern electric car in 1991. Noel Perrin later wrote about his trip in *Solo: Life with an Electric Car.* Perrin was happy with his car's speed on flat land. The car could go 50 miles per hour easily. It went up to

60 miles between charges. For short bursts, the car could even reach 60 miles per hour.

16   But going up a steep hill, the car could barely reach 30 miles per hour. Worse, it ran out of power very quickly.

17   Each time Perrin stopped to recharge, he had big problems. There were no charging stations along the highways. So Perrin had to plug his car into regular outlets. At best, recharging took four hours. Sometimes it took twice that time. That meant that Perrin could travel only about 100 miles a day.

18   The same year, someone else drove an electric car for 24 hours straight under special conditions. Recharging was much quicker. This car went more than 600 miles.

19   In 1992, an electric vehicle did even better with a new charging station. A small electric truck was driven around a race track. Every 60 miles or so, it pulled into the station. A computer controlled the recharging. Each time, the job took less

Will gas stations become a thing of the past if electric cars take over the roads?

than 20 minutes. The truck traveled 831.8 miles in 24 hours, a new world record.

PLANNING AHEAD

20 Could we have fast charging stations—or electricity pumps—along the roads? These would give electric cars the range they need. But such pumps would cause new problems.

21 Electric power companies have more than enough energy at night. Electric cars that are recharged at night could use that energy. But suppose that they needed to

recharge during the day. Then they would need to stop at electricity pumps. The power companies would have to put out more energy. So the power companies would do more polluting, since coal is used to make electricity. That wouldn't help.

22   In short, there is little chance that your next car will be an electric. But each step takes researchers a little further. Why not plan ahead? It may be time to start an electric car savings fund. ♦

QUESTIONS

1. About what year did cars first run on electric batteries?

2. How fast could the first electrics go?

3. What new addition to gas-powered cars made them more popular than electric- or steam-powered cars?

4. Name two things that made Noel Perrin unhappy with his electric car.

5. What was the 1992 world record for distance traveled in 24 hours?

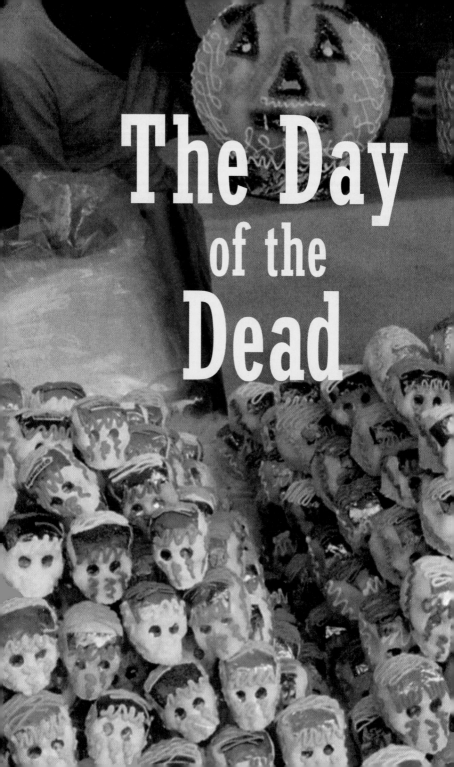

The Day
of the
Dead

How would you feel if you received a candy skull with your name on it?

1 The Day of the Dead sounds frightening or sad. But in Mexico, it is a happy day. It is a day for eating and drinking with your family members—even those who have died.

GETTING READY

2 The Day of the Dead is November 2nd. It is also known as All Souls' Day. To get ready for it, bakers make special loaves of sweet bread. Sometimes the loaves are in the shape of a skull. Little pieces of bread lie across each loaf to look like bones.

Cheerfully decorated skulls are lined up for sale in the market.

3   You can buy candy in the shape of a skull, too. The sugar candy skulls come in all sizes. Some are tiny, and others are bigger than your head. They are decorated with circles of colored paper covering the eyeholes. You can get a candy skull with your name spelled out across the forehead in gold letters. Mothers and fathers like to buy one for each of their children. As a gift, a young man might buy a candy skull with his girlfriend's name on it.

FOOD AND FUN

4 In Mexico, the Day of the Dead is a big holiday. Food stalls line the streets. People walk along eating and enjoying the day.

5   Some towns hold parades. These parades look more like funeral processions. The marchers even carry a coffin. But the people along the streets look happy, and they are laughing. Suddenly the coffin pops open! A person dressed as a skeleton sits up and waves to everyone.

At home, people decorate special altars in celebration of the Day of the Dead.

A TIME TO REMEMBER

6 Although it is a happy event, the Day of the Dead is also a serious one. People set up altars in their homes. They decorate them with flowers, food, and candles. On these altars, the people also place religious symbols, skeletons, and pictures of relatives who have died. All these things show how the people view life and death. Everyone goes to church at some time during the day. They pray for the souls of their loved ones who have died.

Women decorate the graves with marigold petals, the flower of the dead.

7   As night falls, people bring baskets of food and flowers to the churches. There the flowers and food are blessed. Then the people walk, often with musicians, to the cemetery. They go to the graves where members of their family are buried.

8   By the light of lanterns, they decorate the graves with flowers and wreaths. The flower that people bring most often is the marigold. In Mexico, the marigold is the flower of the dead. The women pick the petals off the flowers. They arrange hundreds of the yellow petals in the form of a cross on each grave.

9	Next, they unfold tablecloths that have been washed and ironed for this day. They spread out the tablecloths on the graves. Then they lay out the food they have brought.

TOGETHER AGAIN

10	The women light tall, white candles and put them on the graves. Then the families settle in and wait in the darkness. They have only the candles for light. They wait for the souls of their loved ones to come back to be with them. On this day, they believe, the spirits of the dead come home.

A decorated cemetery is ready for the evening's celebration.

This grandmother and her grandchildren have decorated their family graves with flowers.

11 They are not frightened or sad. They enjoy the feeling that all of their family is together for one special night each year.

12 Morning comes. The candles have burned out. The families eat the food they have set out. Then they begin the walk home, tired but happy.

A Lasting Tradition

13 This is a tradition[1] thousands of years old. In Mexico before Columbus, the Aztec

---

[1] tradition: the handing down of information, beliefs, or customs through family lines

people were in power. They always placed food in the grave as someone was buried.

14   After Columbus came, Mexico was taken over by the country of Spain. The people in this land became Christians. But they did not give up their tradition. They simply changed it to fit their Christian beliefs. And they began to celebrate it as the Day of the Dead. The people of Mexico have kept alive their great feeling for this holiday. It is as strong today as if time had never passed. ♦

QUESTIONS

1. Why do the people of Mexico celebrate the Day of the Dead?

2. What things do families bring to the cemetery?

3. Why do people use marigolds to decorate the graves?

4. Why do people stay all night long in the cemetery?

The Great
DEPRESSION

A Dust Bowl refugee family pauses on the road between Austin and Dallas, Texas, in 1936.

How did President Franklin Delano Roosevelt make sure that people would have some money for their old age?

1   Today, many of us wish we had more money. But in the 1930s, nearly everyone was in deep money trouble. During the worst times, 14 million people were out of work. Those who did have jobs were paid only pennies. Those terrible years were called the Great Depression.[1]

TROUBLE BREWING

2   The trouble started in the 1920s. Most of those years, everything seemed to be fine. But things were not as good as they seemed. Farmers were not getting fair prices for crops. Coal mining, railroad, and clothing businesses were having a hard time. And too many people were getting bank loans they could not pay off.

---

[1] Great Depression: the period of very low business activity and loss of money worldwide brought on by the stock market crash of 1929

3   Then, in 1929, prices of stock[2] in American business began to drop. A stock once worth $100 might end up being worth only $3. On October 29, 1929, the stock market "crashed" to an all-time low. It was called Black Tuesday. Anyone who owned stocks lost a great deal of money. Suddenly, many rich people were poor.

HARD TIMES

4   That was the start of the Great Depression. Many companies went out of business. Millions of workers lost their jobs. When people went to get their money, they found the banks were closed. There was no welfare, unemployment checks, or social security. Millions of people went broke. The same thing was happening in other countries, too.

FROM BAD TO WORSE

5   President Herbert Hoover promised that better times were "just around the corner." He didn't think the government should

---

[2] stock: part of a company that is divided among its owners

Unemployed squatters[3] share a meal near their shack on the west side of Chicago.

step in. But over the next three years, wages fell for those who still had jobs. Prices also fell, but low prices didn't help. Most people were lucky to pay for food and rent. Some families ate "cracker soup" for dinner. Others sorted through garbage for food.

6   Many families lost their homes. They built shacks out of boxes, tin, and old car parts. They slept under newspapers. Soup

---

[3] squatters: ones who settle on land without right or title or payment of rent

Jobless people line up for hand-outs of free bread and coffee in New York City.

kitchens and bread lines were set up. Some children stopped going to school because they didn't have clothes to wear. Men out of work stood on the street selling apples for five cents. Others begged in the street. Many people who had lost hope killed themselves.

7   The weather made matters even worse. In 1930, there was little rain. The land

from South Dakota to Texas to Illinois—called the Dust Bowl—became as dry as sand. Then, in 1931 and 1932, dust storms blew whole farms away. Sand got into food and water. People stayed indoors. They stuffed cloth and paper into any holes in their houses so the wind could not get in.

8   A few years later, there was too much rain. Eleven large rivers flooded. In Ohio, 500,000 homes were washed away. Towns along the great rivers were washed out.

THE NEW DEAL

9   Herbert Hoover ran for president again in 1932. But he lost to Franklin Delano Roosevelt. President Roosevelt believed that the government should step in to end the depression. His plan was called the New Deal. It started a number of new programs.

10   Roosevelt and Congress put new government controls on banks and the stock market. They sent out $500 million to help the poorest people. They set up

President Franklin Delano Roosevelt
started creating jobs for needy people.

jobs for people to plant trees and build dams and power plants. To drive up farm prices, they paid farmers to plant less. To help people keep their homes and farms, they gave government loans. They worked with companies to hire more workers.

MORE PROGRAMS

11 Then the Works Progress Administration, or WPA, began. Under this new program, people built schools, hospitals, bridges, roads, airports, and government buildings.

It also paid people to paint, sculpt,[4] write, dance, and make music. Even today, many post offices, schools, and parks have works by WPA artists.

12   In 1935, Social Security began. Workers paid a tax so they would have money in their old age. Social Security paid women and children who had lost a working man in the family. It also started a state welfare program and an unemployment plan. People who were out of work would get some money until they found another job.

13   President Roosevelt helped the country make it through the Great Depression. Not everyone liked what he did. Yet Roosevelt was the only president to win the office of president four times.

CHASING AWAY THE BLUES

14 Movies filled with music and dance helped people to smile through the worst of the 1930s. Hollywood came into its own and radio became a big hit. People heard Bing

---

[4] sculpt: to make a carving or molding out of a hard substance

A young Bob Hope brought smiles to thousands with his humorous radio shows.

Crosby sing. They enjoyed listening to radio shows such as "The Shadow" and "The Lone Ranger." They laughed with Bob Hope or listened to new music by Benny Goodman, the "King of Swing." But the most famous song of the depression was "Brother, Can You Spare a Dime?"

COMING BACK

15 Slowly, America crawled out of the Great Depression. But Roosevelt's programs alone could not end this awful time. When

World War II broke out, America needed its factories and farms again. Men went off to fight, while women went to work. The war got America back on its feet.

16   The country has been up and down since the Great Depression. But the laws passed under Roosevelt helped make sure that it can never happen again. ◆

QUESTIONS

1. What year did the stock market crash?

2. Who was the president at the time?

3. What was the New Deal?

4. What is Social Security, and when did it start?

5. How many times did Roosevelt win the presidency?

6. Besides the New Deal, what helped end the Great Depression?

When Anna Pavlova danced in New York in 1910, people said "she soars as though on wings."

Which famous ballet dancer was called the "god of the dance"?

Great Names in Dance

1 Ballet is a high form of dance. It grew out of Italy and France as far back as the Middle Ages. Ballet steps were first written down in 1581. Ballet came to Russia in the mid-1800s.

2 To be a great ballet dancer, a person must practice very hard. Over the years, many dancers have done this. Some became quite famous.

3 The first famous dancer in the United States was John Durang. He first danced in Philadelphia in 1785. But that was long before most Americans had ever heard of ballet.

DANCERS FROM EUROPE

4 Dance was much bigger in Europe then. Ballet steps were being written down in

Austrian dancer Fanny Elssler was the first popular ballet star in 1840s America.

books. The art of dance grew. In the early 1800s, a dancer named Marie Anne de Dupis [day Doo•pee'] became famous in France. She was the first dancer to wear skirts short enough to show her feet. She wanted people to see what her dancing feet could do.

5   It was not until 1840 that Americans saw great dancers from another country.

Fanny Elssler [Ehls'·ler] came from Austria to New York in 1840. She danced all over America for two years. The U.S. Congress even gave her a big party. Because of Fanny Elssler, Americans became interested in ballet.

ISADORA DUNCAN

6 Isadora Duncan was the first American dance star. She learned all the ballet steps

Isadora Duncan, the first American dance star, began as a ballet dancer. But she went on to create her own modern dance style.

and moves. She could do them well. But she wanted to put more of herself into her dancing. She wanted to move in new ways. Her style did not go over well in Chicago and New York. So she left for Europe in 1898. There she opened dance schools in France, Germany, and Russia. She also became famous for her wild lifestyle. Duncan's style of modern dance started as ballet but broke away from it.

THE GREAT PAVLOVA

7 In 1910, Anna Pavlova came to New York from Russia. People said, "She does not dance; she soars as though on wings." Many thought that no dancer ever worked harder than Pavlova. She danced 15 hours a day, each day. Perhaps the most famous dance of all is "The Dying Swan." Anna Pavlova was the one who made it famous.

8 In 1916 a new Russian ballet company first came to America. Started in 1909, it had a French name, the Ballets Russes [Roose]. Anna Pavlova danced with that

This rare private picture of Anna Pavlova shows her with one of her pet swans. Her most famous dance was "The Dying Swan."

company for about a year. After dancing all over the world, Pavlova died in 1931.

FROM THE BALLETS RUSSES

9 A number of other great dancers rose out of the famous Ballets Russes. Vaslav Nijinsky [Vaht'•slahf Nuh•zhin'•skee] was one. He was called the "god of the dance." To this day, many view Nijinsky as the greatest of all ballet dancers. He was the son of two dancers. By age 17, he was already a star in

Russia. For the next 12 years, he danced with the Ballets Russes all over Europe and the United States. Then, when he was only 29, he left the world of ballet. He lived a quiet life until he died in 1950.

10   Michel Fokine [Mee•shel' Fo•keen'] also danced with the Ballets Russes. But he is better known for composing and arranging dances. He wrote "The Dying Swan" for Pavlova in 1905. The Ballets Russes company broke up in 1929. Fokine was one of its members who stayed in the

Margot Fonteyn and Rudolph Nureyev pose after dancing together in "Romeo et Juliet."

United States. He became an American citizen in 1932, though he worked mainly in Europe. He died in 1942.

Famous Partners

11 Rudolf Nureyev [Noo'·ray·yuf] was born in what is now Russia in 1938. He began to study ballet at age 11. As a young man, he danced with the Kirov Ballet. Americans first saw him on TV in 1962. That same year, Nureyev went to England. He joined the Royal Ballet in London. There, he began to dance with Margot Fonteyn [Mar'·goh Fahn·tane']. She was already more than 40 years old. But she and Nureyev danced together for many years. They became the best known pair of dancers in the world. Margot Fonteyn died in 1991. After performing the world over, acting in movies, and leading a dance company, Nureyev died in 1993.

Mikhail Baryshnikov

12 Mikhail Baryshnikov [Mee·kale' Bah·rizh'·nih·kawv] also came out of the Kirov Ballet. He was born in Latvia. He later

Mikhail Baryshnikov's strong, smooth moves make dance look easy.

studied dance in what is now St. Petersburg. In 1974, he was dancing in Canada. When the other Kirov dancers went home, Baryshnikov stayed behind. He felt he could do more as a dancer by leaving his country. Soon he joined the American Ballet Theatre. He tried out many new ideas in dance. He also wrote dances and starred in movies.

13   For a short time, Baryshnikov danced with the New York City Ballet. Then he was director of the American Ballet Theatre

from 1980 to 1989. Many people think of Baryshnikov as the greatest male ballet dancer of his time. His strong, smooth moves make dance look easy.

BEAUTY TO BEHOLD

14 Many great ballet dancers have graced stages all over the world. Words cannot show the beauty of their art. For a clearer idea of these world-class talents, watch them on TV or video. As the saying goes, one picture is worth a thousand words. ♦

QUESTIONS

1. Who was America's first famous ballet dancer?

2. Which dancer made ballet popular in the United States?

3. Who made the dance "The Dying Swan" famous?

4. Which ballet dancer is often said to be the greatest of all time?

5. Which dancer directed the American Ballet Theatre for nearly 10 years?

Why did Chief Meyers quit his studies—
all expenses paid—at one of the
best schools in the country?

Pride
of the
Giants

1 John "Chief" Meyers was a major league baseball player about 90 years ago. He was proud to be in baseball. He was just as proud of his Native American heritage.[1]

2 The Cahuillas [Kah•hoo•ee'•yuz] were one of the tribes of the Mission Indians of southern California. They lived high in the peaks of the San Jacinto [Juh•seen'•toe] Mountains. John Tortes Meyers was born in a Cahuilla village in 1880. His people were known as a proud and independent tribe. It is no wonder that Meyers grew up to be that way, too.

---

[1] heritage: something handed down from the past

By 1910, Chief Meyers had become the Giants'
regular catcher.

Following a Dream

3 When Meyers was about 11, the family moved to the city of Riverside. He attended public schools there. When he finished high school, college was far from his mind. His heart was set on playing baseball.

4 Meyers's skills were so good that several semiprofessional[2] [seh•mi•proh•feh'•shun•ul] teams hired him as a catcher. Meyers made no secret of his Native American background. He was aware of the prejudice against minorities in those days. But he had pride in his heritage. Soon he got the nickname of "Chief."

Help from Abroad

5 In 1904, Chief Meyers's life took an interesting turn. His baseball team was playing in Albuquerque [Al'•buh•ker•kee], New Mexico. That's where he met an all-American football player named Ralph Glaze. Glaze was a student at Dartmouth College in New Hampshire.

---

[2] semiprofessional: doing an activity for pay but not as full-time work

6   Glaze told Meyers about a scholarship at Dartmouth. Who had set up the scholarship? An earl in England! In the 1700s, the school was known as Moor's Indian Charity School. The teachers were English missionaries [mih'•shun•air•eez]. The earl of Dartmouth heard about the school. He sent money for a special scholarship fund. The scholarship could go only to a Native American who was a good enough student to study there. The school was later renamed for the earl.

7   Meyers put in for the scholarship and was accepted. He could not play baseball for the school because he was not an amateur[3] [am'•uh•cher]. When school was out for the summer, he played for Harrisburg, Pennsylvania, in the Tri-State League. He had planned to return to Dartmouth at the end of the summer. But he was called home to the bedside of his sick mother. When her health improved, it

---

[3] amateur: one who takes part in an activity for pleasure, not for money

was too late for him to return to school. He regretted that for the rest of his life.

PLAY BALL

8 The best thing Chief Meyers could pursue was another career in baseball. At first, he played for minor league teams in Montana and Minnesota. In 1908, he joined the National League's New York Giants.

9 At that time, John McGraw was the team's manager. Meyers greatly admired him. He felt that McGraw had changed the public's feeling toward baseball players. In the early part of the century, players were

Fans watch a game at the Polo Grounds, home field of the New York Giants.

Chief Meyers is shown at bat. His lifetime batting average was .291.

not always treated with respect. As an example, they weren't allowed in the better hotels for out-of-town games. But McGraw didn't go along with that. He paid for his players to stay at the best hotels.

HAIL TO THE CHIEF

10 Chief Meyers also had great respect for umpire Bill Klem and Giants pitcher Christy Mathewson. By 1910, Meyers became the team's regular catcher. His highest batting average was .358, in 1912. The team won pennants in 1911, 1912, and 1913.

11   In 1916, Meyers was traded to the Brooklyn Robins (later renamed the Dodgers). Meyers retired the following year. His lifetime batting average was .291. His top salary was about $6,000 a year.

It's All in the Game

12 The subject of salary came up in an interview when Chief Meyers was in his 80s. Meyers said that today's players are businessmen. "They've got agents and outside interests and all that sort of thing. We played for money, too. Naturally. That's how we made our living. But mostly we played just for the love of it. . . . Most of us would have paid *them* just to let us play. We loved baseball."

13   In that same interview, Meyers compared himself to an old warrior chief of the great Six Nations. The chief had said, "I am like an old hemlock.[4] My head is still high, but the winds of close to 100 winters have whistled through my branches, and I have been witness to many

---

[4] hemlock: a kind of evergreen tree

wondrous and many tragic things. My eyes perceive[5] the present, but my roots are imbedded[6] deeply in the grandeur of the past." Chief Meyers died in 1971 at the age of 90. ♦

QUESTIONS

1. Where does the Cahuilla tribe come from?

2. Why was John Meyers nicknamed "Chief"?

3. What year did Meyers join the New York Giants?

4. Why did Meyers admire the Giants' manager, John McGraw?

5. What position did Meyers play most often with the Giants?

---

[5] perceive: see
[6] imbedded: set solidly within

Would you like to live in a land with dark days and "white nights"?

Dark Days

1   Days are light. Nights are dark. That's how most of the world thinks of day and night. But the people of Iceland and parts of Norway, Sweden, and Finland don't think that way. To them, winter days are as dark as night.

2   The sun is what makes daylight. When the sun drops below the horizon[1] of any place on Earth, the sky becomes dark. To most people in the world, that means night. But in winter, in northern Scandinavia [Skan·dih·nay'·vee·ah], the sun never makes it above the horizon at all. So, there is no daylight. Days are dark, just like nights.

---

[1] horizon: the line where Earth or sea seems to meet the sky

THE ARCTIC CIRCLE

3 Scandinavia is really five countries: Denmark, Finland, Iceland, Norway, and Sweden. Iceland and parts of Norway, Sweden, and Finland fall within the Arctic [Ark'•tik] Circle. In those northern places, days are dark for 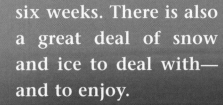 six weeks. There is also a great deal of snow and ice to deal with— and to enjoy.

4 Cold, dark winters have always played a big part in the lives of Scandinavian people. This is seen in many of the folktales of the land. The trolls[2] of the old stories hated sun, but the people loved it. The frost giants of other tales stood for the force of the harsh winters. They fought against all that was good. In story after story, the faraway light of summer stood for hope.

---

[2] trolls: dwarfs or giants of folklore who live in caves or hills

AUTUMN-WINTER

5 In the northern parts of Scandinavia, there are three winters: autumn-winter, high-winter, and spring-winter. Autumn-winter is in October and November, the elk-hunting season. Some say this first winter is the worst. The beautiful snow has not yet come. There is still some daylight. Yet everyone knows the darkness is on its way.

HIGH-WINTER FUN

6 The last day with any light at all is in December. This is the beginning of high-winter. The snow and ice come, but they are beautiful in the dark. The moon and stars seem brighter against the snow. This is also the time of the northern lights. Bits of the sun break off and pass through the sky as red, blue, and white arcs of light.

7 During high-winter, many northern Scandinavians go south, like the birds. But those who stay home in the dark can have plenty of fun. This is the time when friends get together most often. There are plays and music to enjoy. And there are the

many winter sports for which the Scandinavian countries are famous.

8   Children learning to walk learn to ski at the same time. Three or more feet of snow cover the ground every day. People cross-country ski to get where they want to go. Children may go to school in the dark and come home in the dark. But they also have days off to go skiing. Ice skating is a favorite winter activity. Ice-hole fishing

Cross-country skiing is the best way to get around when everything is covered with lots of snow.

keeps many people busy. Iceboating and ice hockey are popular sports.

SPECIAL PROBLEMS

9 But the winter is not all fun and games. There are a number of winter problems to deal with. For many people, the "winter blues" come with the darkness. Many people have trouble sleeping, even though it is dark. Everyone has to dress in warm, heavy clothes and boots just to go outside. Everyone wears a fur hat.

10 The cost of heat is high. To keep the heat in and save money, windows have

This typical Danish house has a steeply slanting roof so that snow will slide off, not pile up.

Small windows with shutters, heavy doors, and thick walls help keep out the winter cold.

three layers of glass. Some windows are made with metal-plated glass to bounce indoor heat back into the home. To keep out the cold, walls are very thick. Some doors are so heavy they are hard to open. Nearly every home has a fireplace or stove with a damper[3] to keep out cold air.

A WAY OF LIFE

11 Northern Scandinavians make up for the darkness by making their own light. Though the sky is dark, all kinds of bright

[3]damper: a valve or plate used to control drafts

The northern countries' dark days end on January 21 with four minutes of sunlight.

lights flood the towns. If you flew over Scandinavia during the winter, you would see many, many lights. The number of lights is high for the number of people living in this land.

12   While all of this may seem odd, the northern people are used to their dark winters. "The sun is a strange object in the sky that you rarely see in winter," says one woman from Finland. "I don't think much about the darkness. It seems normal." Some people in this land even say a baby born in the winter is two nights old, rather than two days old.

13   On January 21, the sun rises high enough to give four minutes of daylight. The people of northern Scandinavia have parties to welcome the light.

SPRING-WINTER

14 March and April mark spring-winter, the third winter season. Little by little, the days grow longer. But the snow and ice melt into brown slush. Roads are covered with mud. Spring-winter is not a pretty time. The long winter finally gives way to the short, beautiful summer. The weather is warm but not hot. This is called the time of flowers. By July, the northern days are so long that there is no darkness at all.

These are the "white nights." That's why the Arctic Circle is called the "land of the midnight sun."

15   To the people of northern Scandinavia, summer is very special. They get out and enjoy it. Or they go on holiday for months

During summer days in Scandinavia, there is no night at all.

Flowers blooming in a window are a sign that summer's long days are on the way.

at a time. They know that soon enough the dark days of winter will be upon them once again. ◆

QUESTIONS

1. Which countries make up Scandinavia?

2. Name the three kinds of winter in the Arctic Circle.

3. How do the people of this land make up for the darkness during winter?

4. What are the northern lights?

5. Why is the Arctic Circle called "the land of the midnight sun"?

Nellie Bly waves good-bye as she prepares to set off on her record-breaking trip around the world.

Why would a newspaper reporter want to stay at a home for the mentally ill?

THE
FABULOUS
MISS BLY

1   In 1890, New York held a parade in honor of Elizabeth Cochrane [Kock'•run]. Was she a movie star? An astronaut [as'•tro•naht]? A visiting princess? No. She was a newspaper reporter. She was about 23 years old. And she had just circled the globe in 72 days.

2   In those days, many young women had hard, dull jobs. Their pay was low. Almost all good jobs went to men. After all, people said, a woman's place is in the home. In 1885, the *Pittsburgh Dispatch* printed an editorial[1] about working women. It said

---

[1] editorial: a newspaper or magazine article that gives the opinions of its editors or publishers

that women could not do a good job outside the home.

Look Out, World!

3 Elizabeth Cochrane read the article. She was young and eager for adventure. The article made her angry. She wrote to the *Dispatch*. Women, she said, could do many jobs well. It was wrong to waste their talents. The paper printed her letter. Then Cochrane asked for a job as a reporter. The editor liked her letter. So he gave her a try.

4 Cochrane wrote under another name. She chose Nellie Bly. "Nellie Bly" is the name of a song by Stephen Foster, an American songwriter who lived in the 1800s.

Travel to Mexico

5 Nellie Bly's first reports told about the hard lives of other working women. She wrote about the slums of Pittsburgh. She wrote about divorce. She got readers excited about her topics.

Nellie Bly loved adventure. Her first trip as a writer took her to Mexico.

6 The *Dispatch* saw how popular Bly's work was. So in 1887 the paper sent her to Mexico. For six months, Bly traveled around Mexico. She wrote reports about all that she saw.

7   In those days, few people saw other countries. There were no movies or TV shows about far-off lands. So almost everything in Bly's reports was new to her readers. They were eager to learn about Mexico. Later, Bly published her reports in a book called *Six Months in Mexico*.

Bly Tells All

8 Soon after Bly came home to Pittsburgh, she moved to New York. She had a new job with a larger paper. She then worked for the *New York World*.

9   Bly's first big topic in New York was insane asylums[2] [uh•sy'•lums]. Most often, the city asylums made little news. People with mental illnesses were just "put away" and forgotten. But how well were patients treated? Bly wanted to find out.

10   Bly knew that visitors are always shown the best things. She wanted to see the worst things, too. So she pretended to be

---

[2] insane asylums: hospital-like places for the care of mentally ill persons

insane. She was sent to a New York asylum as a patient.

11   Inside, Bly learned that patients were often mistreated. Many were dirty and hungry. They were left for long times without care. Instead of getting better, patients got worse.

12   Two weeks later, Bly was out of the asylum. But the outcome of her daring stunt lasted for years. Her reports about asylums were first printed in the *World*. Later, they came out as a book called *Ten Days in a Madhouse*. Readers were shocked by what she wrote. They cried for changes. Because of Bly, life got better for patients in New York asylums.

THE BIGGEST TRIP OF ALL

13 Nellie Bly had proved she was a great reporter. But she still wanted adventure. A book gave her the idea for her greatest success. *Around the World in Eighty Days* was a popular book in 1889. It tells the tale of Phileas [Fil'•ee•us] Fogg, a noted English

gentleman. On a bet, he travels around the world in just 80 days. Few people believed the trip was possible. Bly thought she could make the trip even faster.

14   At first, the *World* would not let her try. The idea was crazy. No one could go around the world in so few days! And for a woman, there would be added danger. But Bly kept asking. Finally, her boss told her to go ahead. He knew Bly loved adventure. Besides, the trip could make both her and the paper famous.

15   Bly packed a single bag. Then she set off. On November 14, 1889, at 9:40 A.M., her ship left New Jersey. Bly first landed in England. Then she went on to France. There she met Jules Verne, the writer of *Around the World in Eighty Days*. After Verne wished her good luck, Bly left for Hong Kong.

A RACE AGAINST TIME

16 Nellie Bly traveled by ship, train, horse, handcart, and burro.[3] Wherever she went,

---

[3] burro: a small donkey often used as a pack animal

Racing against time, Nellie Bly took a train from San Franciso back to New Jersey.

she wrote. She kept an exact record of what she saw and did. Bly planned to share her adventures with others. She wanted her readers to feel as if they had traveled along with her.

17   When Bly's ship from Hong Kong reached San Francisco, she was famous. The *World* sent a train to meet her. It would bring her to New Jersey as fast as it could. Even so, crowds met the train at each stop. Everyone wanted to see the young world traveler.

When she was older, Nellie Bly worked to help women get the right to vote.

18   At last, the train reached New Jersey. Bly jumped from it on January 25, 1890, at 3:31 P.M. She had circled Earth in exactly 72 days, 6 hours, and 11 minutes. The waiting crowd cheered. A few days later, New York greeted her. Fireworks went off. Brass bands played. A parade marched down Broadway.

19   Of course, Bly reported on her trip in the *World*. She also wrote *Nellie Bly's Book: Around the World in Seventy-Two Days*. This was her most popular book.

OTHER ADVENTURES

20 Nellie Bly kept up her writing until 1895. Then she married Robert Seaman, a very rich man. After he died, she ran his business. But her gift was for news, not business. By 1920, she was writing again.

21 Nellie Bly died in 1922. By then, planes carried people over land and seas. Bly's speed record was broken. Yet Bly's boldness is still a model. And her spirit of adventure will never age. ♦

QUESTIONS

1. Why was Nellie Bly angry when she read the article in the *Pittsburgh Dispatch*?

2. Name some topics of Bly's first reports with the newspaper.

3. How and why did Bly enter the New York insane asylum as a patient?

4. Why did Bly want to travel around the world?

*Why do we feel more alert
when we drink coffee?*

A Good Cup of Coffee

1 What do you drink when you feel tired or when you just want to take a break? Many people like a cup of hot coffee.

2 Coffee comes from beans. They grow on trees with green shiny leaves. Coffee trees grow only where it is warm all year round. They also need lots of rain. Coffee trees grow high in the mountains. The best trees are in South America and Africa.

WHERE IT COMES FROM

3 Coffee trees grow on plantations.[1] Workers prune the trees so that they stay under 15 feet tall. This makes it easy to pick the beans.

---

[1] plantations: areas where groups of plants and trees are cared for

A steaming cup of coffee is the way many people start their morning.

Coffee berries turn from green to red as they ripen over 6 to 14 months.

4   The beans start as pretty, white flowers. When the flowers drop, bunches of green coffee berries start to grow. Each berry has two beans in it. The berries turn red as they ripen. It takes from 6 to 14 months for them to get ripe. On some plantations, all the berries are picked at once. But for the very best coffee, workers pick only the ripe berries.

GREEN GOLD

5 Picking the berries is the first step. The berries go through many more steps before they can be made into coffee. The berries are spread out in the sun to dry. Next, workers rake them to be sure they all get dry. Then they put the berries into a machine to rub off the outer hulls. The beans remain, but they are still green. The workers call them green gold.

6 The coffee beans are shipped to other countries. They still are not ready to be made into coffee. Then they are roasted until they turn brown. Then the beans are put through big rollers that grind them. Most coffee that we drink does not come from just one kind of bean. It is made from a blend of beans from different kinds of trees. Some people work as trained tasters. They sip the coffees to see how they should be blended. Then the coffee is packed in airtight containers. It is finally ready to go to the stores.

LOOK ALIVE!

7 Why do people drink coffee when they are tired? Coffee contains a drug called caffeine[2] [ka•feen']. By itself, caffeine is white, like sugar. Caffeine stimulates[3] the body's nervous system. This makes a person feel more alert. It also helps the brain work a little faster.

8 Caffeine also stimulates the heart and the stomach. This is bad for some people. It keeps some coffee drinkers awake at night. For these reasons, many people drink decaffeinated [dee•kaf'•fi•nay•tud] coffee. This brew has had much of the caffeine removed.

9 While they are still green, coffee beans are treated with a chemical. This chemical joins itself to the caffeine. Then the chemical is steamed out, taking the caffeine with it. Like regular coffee beans, these beans are dried, roasted, and ground. Both kinds of beans can also be used to make instant coffee.

[2] caffeine: a bitter drug that makes the body feel active
[3] stimulates: makes active or more active

Coffee drinking has been popular for a long time. This picture shows an open-air coffee stall in Paris around 1850.

HOW IT BEGAN

10 We drink billions of cups of coffee each year. People in the United States drink one-third of all the coffee in the world! How did it all start? Coffee trees first grew in Africa. People there chewed the berries to stay awake. Then they found that they could grind the beans to make a drink. Coffee became very popular. Trees were planted in many other places.

One hundred years later, Parisians are shown still enjoying their coffee in this 1954 photo.

11   There were no coffee trees in North America or South America. Around 1700, a young French soldier brought one tree from a garden in France. He carried it to North America on a sailing ship. It was a long, hard trip. The people on the ship began to run out of drinking water. But the young soldier shared his water with the tree, and he kept it alive. When he got to North America, he planted the tree. Almost all the coffee trees in this part of the world come from that one tree!

A POPULAR CUSTOM

12 Throughout history, thousands of lively talks about art and politics have taken place in coffeehouses. And they are popular places today for the same reasons. Important decisions have been made over cups of coffee. There are even songs about coffee. Its good taste and smell has placed coffee among the most popular of all hot drinks. Whether taken black, creamed, weak, or strong, it seems that coffee is here to stay. ♦

QUESTIONS

1. Where are the best coffee trees in the world?

2. How long does it take for coffee berries to ripen?

3. How is caffeine taken out of coffee?

4. How did coffee first come to North America?

Janet Hernandez's troubles started when she bought a used car. Was it haunted?

What would make you believe in ghosts?

Tales for a Stormy Night

1 Do you joke about ghosts? Maybe you just wonder about them. Of course, you might be someone who believes in them.

2 Not long ago, a magazine had an idea for Halloween. It asked readers to send in ghost tales. More than 500 people sent them in. Their stories were not made up. The strange things they related had really happened.

THE HAUNTED CAR

3 Many people wrote about haunted houses. But only one story was about a haunted car! Janet Hernandez bought a used car.

While washing it, she found three holes. Could they be bullet holes? "Who cares," Janet thought. She filled them and painted over them. The car looked as good as new. But every time she drove, the passenger door would fly open. She had it checked many times. Nothing was wrong with the door. One day Janet's father used rope to tie it shut. That same day they drove past a cemetery. The door flew open, rope and all! That's when Janet made up her mind to sell the car.

MESSAGE FROM BEYOND

4 Carolyn Young believes that the dead have ways to talk. After a fall that broke her ankle, Carolyn's mother didn't want to live. When she died, Carolyn and her husband sorted her mother's things. Her television set had always worked fine. So they took it home. When they turned it on, it went black. After having the TV repaired, Carolyn tried to use it. This time it began to smoke. She was afraid it would explode. Her mother had never liked

Carolyn Young believes that her TV set was possessed by the spirit of her dead mother.

Carolyn's husband. Carolyn and her husband talked about the problems they were having with the television. Maybe her mother was still showing how she felt about her son-in-law. Carolyn and her husband didn't want to fix the television again. As they moved it to the trash, one leg of the set broke. It was the right leg— the same one Carolyn's mother had broken before she died.

Did Boomer the cat come back from the grave to take his revenge on Michael Fadden?

PET PEEVE

5 Do pets also "talk" from the grave? Michael Fadden thinks so. His wife loved cats, but he didn't. One day she brought home a cat named Boomer. Michael and Boomer didn't hit it off. Boomer liked to tear Michael's ties with its claws. The owner of the building said pets could not live there. So Boomer was sent to live with Michael's in-laws. Two weeks later, Boomer was killed by a truck. Late one night, Michael heard a noise. It came from the closet. He

looked inside but saw nothing. The next morning, Michael had a surprise. As he put on his tie, he saw it was torn by claws!

A Musical Ghost

6 One woman's story was about strange music. Patricia Bracker grew up in a 100-year-old house. One night she heard music. It sounded like the song "Ten Little Indians." Her mother told her to turn off the music. But no radio or stereo was turned on. Years later, Patricia talked to a granddaughter of the first owner of the

Patricia Bracker heard ghostly music. Was her old house still occupied by its first owner?

house. Her grandfather had played the violin. The granddaughter said, "Before he died, he lived in your bedroom. He tuned his violin at night by playing 'Ten Little Indians.'"

7　　Think about these "real" ghost stories. Have they changed your mind about ghosts? No matter. But listen carefully at night. You might hear strange sounds. You might even see shadowy shapes. Just don't let them scare you. ♦

QUESTIONS

1. How did Janet Hernandez's father try to fix the car door?

2. What were some of the problems that Carolyn Young had with her mother's television?

3. What did Michael Fadden find in his closet the morning after he heard a noise there?

4. What story did Patricia Bracker hear about the first owner of her house?

GLOSSARY

ALL KINDS OF CATS
Pages 4–13
breeds: groups of plants or animals that are related by family lines and that have like traits
Ice Age: a time long ago when ice covered most of the Earth
Middle Ages: the time in Europe's history from about A.D. 500 to A.D. 1500
saber-toothed tiger: large cat of long ago with long, curved upper teeth

ELECTRIC CARS
Pages 14–23
pollutes: makes impure

THE DAY OF THE DEAD
Pages 24–31
tradition: the handing down of information, beliefs, or customs through family lines

THE GREAT DEPRESSION
Pages 32–41
Great Depression: the period of very low business activity and loss of money worldwide brought on by the stock market crash of 1929
sculpt: to make a carving or molding out of a hard substance
squatters: ones who settle on land without right or title or payment of rent
stock: part of a company that is divided among its owners

PRIDE OF THE GIANTS
Pages 52–59
amateur: one who takes part in an activity for pleasure, not for money

hemlock: a kind of evergreen tree
heritage: something handed down from the past
imbedded: set solidly within
perceive: see
semiprofessional: doing an activity for pay but not as full-time work

DARK DAYS
Pages 60–69
damper: a valve or plate used to control drafts
horizon: the line where Earth or sea seems to meet the sky
trolls: dwarfs or giants of folklore who live in caves or hills

THE FABULOUS MISS BLY
Pages 70–79
burro: a small donkey often used as a pack animal
editorial: a newspaper or magazine article that gives the opinions of its editors or publishers
insane asylums: hospital-like places for the care of mentally ill persons

A GOOD CUP OF COFFEE
Pages 80–87
caffeine: a bitter drug that makes the body feel active
plantations: areas where groups of plants and trees are cared for
stimulates: makes active or more active

THE CONTEMPORARY READER
VOLUME 1, NUMBERS 1-6

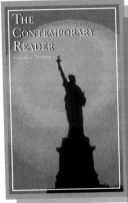

The Contemporary Readers offer nonfiction stories—intriguing, inspiring, and thought provoking—that address current adult issues and interests through lively writing and colorful photography.